WE

WE

poems

April Ossmann

Red Hen Press | *Pasadena, CA*

Book design by Mark E. Cull.

Library of Congress Cataloging-in-Publication Data

Names: Ossmann, April, author.
Title: *We*: poems / April Ossmann.
Description: First edition. | Pasadena, CA: Red Hen Press, 2025.
Identifiers: LCCN 2024018893 (print) | LCCN 2024018894 (ebook) | ISBN
  9781636281728 (trade paperback) | ISBN 9781636282510 (hardcover) | ISBN
  9781636281735 (ebook)
Subjects: LCSH: Poetry. lcgft
Classification: LCC PS3615.S634 W4 2025 (print) | LCC PS3615.S634 (ebook)
  | DDC 811/.6—dc23/eng/20240429
LC record available at https://lccn.loc.gov/2024018893
LC ebook record available at https://lccn.loc.gov/2024018894

The National Endowment for the Arts, the Los Angeles County Arts Commission, the Ahmanson Foundation, the Dwight Stuart Youth Fund, the Max Factor Family Foundation, the Pasadena Tournament of Roses Foundation, the Pasadena Arts & Culture Commission and the City of Pasadena Cultural Affairs Division, the City of Los Angeles Department of Cultural Affairs, the Audrey & Sydney Irmas Charitable Foundation, the Meta & George Rosenberg Foundation, the Albert and Elaine Borchard Foundation, the Adams Family Foundation, Amazon Literary Partnership, the Sam Francis Foundation, and the Mara W. Breech Foundation partially support Red Hen Press.

First Edition
Published by Red Hen Press
www.redhen.org

Acknowledgments:

Grateful acknowledgment is made to the editors of the journals and anthologies who first published the following poems. The poems, sometimes in earlier versions, appeared as follows:

Birchsongs II (Blueline Press): "Autumn Road," "The Force"; *From the Fishouse*: "How to Keep Your Head from Exploding"; *Green Mountains Review*: "The Beyond," "The Knock-Knock Bardo"; *Haiku of Sheltering* (pandemic exhibition at the Highland Center for the Arts): "American Quarantine"; *Interim: A Journal of Poetry & Poetics*: "Corridors," "Dark Suite for My Country," "Knee-Deep"; *The Laurel Review*: "The City of Lost Shoes"; *PoemCity 2016*: "April's Cream Scones, or Saving April from Megalomania"; *Post Road Magazine*: "Non-Partisan" (also included in the CD album, *Garden Dreams,* music by Aaron Marcus, poems voiced by Sam Sanders); *Prairie Schooner*: "I Could Be Driving"; *Roads Taken: Contemporary Vermont Poetry* (Green Writers Press): "Juno's First Fly-By," "What Is Metaphor For?"; *Suffrage and Beyond: Our Voices, Bodies Rising*: video dance & poetry, choreographed by Peggy Brightman: "Peace Hymn for the Republic"; *Third Coast*: "Eclipse."

"We" is in conversation with Walt Whitman's "Song of Myself," "Twenty-First Century Preamble" with the Preamble, to the Constitution, and "Peace Hymn for the Republic" is in conversation with Julia Ward Howe's "Battle Hymn of the Republic." The stones in "Hunger Stones" refer the ones in the Elbe River in the Czech Republic, and *The Central Park Five* refers to Ken Burns' documentary film. "The Force" is dedicated to Ralph Stone and Scott Danyew; and "The Knock-Knock Bardo," to Lisa Bellamy. A big thank you to Nathalie Handal for her generous editorial eye.

Contents

III

WE

Non-Partisan

If I told you
I saw your soul,
would you judge me
inappropriate,
or disbelieve me?
If you asked
for a description,
would I admit
you glowed, golden
as these late
northern afternoons,
whose slanted autumn light
makes green fire
of a backlit tree's
shimmering leaves,
and balances
me perfectly,
on the tightrope
between yearning
and content,
as if I finally understood
what beauty meant
to tell me?

I

We

I celebrate my being, every atom
of myself and you, lamp and mirror

of all that is: I will assume as we,
even if it makes an ass of u or me,

I will love my ass and others I kiss,
as I love every donkey, grass blade,

rhinoceros, bumble bee and monkey—
I will *look through the eyes of the dead,*

and the living, I will give up some virginities
and keep others—and however well

or poorly I sing, I will do it with gladness,
honoring *the procreant urge of the world*

with books—I will sniff some roses,
and gild some lilies, love the sea

and mountains equally, thank
every tree for purifying aspirations—

I will have my loaf and eat it
with loads of butter,

with a thousand crumbs of appreciation
for its texture, grains and flavor,

for all the labor of growing,
harvesting, transporting, baking—

for its making and mine:
April Ossmann, infinite cosmos,

Santa Barbara's daughter—*Yes,*
descended from a saint, as every one

of the world's multitudes—
ascended to the female gender,

the equal of every other,
grateful to my mother and father,

divine as every citizen, refugee, hermit,
immigrant or outcast speeding seagull

overflowing essence—a love
to flood every door from its jamb,

singing, *I am*, multiple, dazzling,
as every woman and man,

every gender we imagine or invent,
every rainbowed event whose ends

dip into the prismatic mystery
we wait life-long to see—

wherein I will learn to play
four-dimensional chess

with my intellect—and not neglect
my body, whose loyal, uncomplaining feet,

wide and long as they are strong,
ballast and carry me wherever

pique or justice, will or love,
peace or imagination inspires—

I will embrace all that transpires:
arms and armpits, legs and cleavages,

belly and back, cheeks,
and brow whose venerable shelf

we imagine as the seat of all our sense,
yet I argue a kind of porous fence,

through which flourishes a wisdom
hidden by the unconscious,

providing access to every mystery
we imagine behind a veil,

though they reside on either side—
we are larger and more divine

than any have yet perceived,
conceived in the wisdom

of a greater love
we should promulgate,

whether in religion
or atheism or agnosticism,

or indecision, in every village
or city, continent or planet,

amid every ethnicity, gender,
sexuality and ability—pardon me,

if I've left any in the dust or ether—
if I must, I'll ride to infamy,

on a horse of every color,
embracing both humility and pride—

Whoever degrades another
degrades me, and whatever

is done or said returns at last to me,
sewn with my own thread,

the weave of which I hope to see,
beautiful as tapestry, clearly

as Penelope, Arachne,
and The Three Fates,

generously as allowed
by my eyes, and soul overflowing,

green as eternity lit by undying fire
no supernova could hope

to outshine. I could go on
for an eon, but let us say, *Divine*,

until we believe it, until we live it
within and beyond the body,

creating the atoms of every moment
in the time-space continuum, shivering

the timbers of history and herstory,
adding our light to the cosmos as if we owned it.

Autumn Road

No clinging autumn mist
          or foreboding
              will deny me
the brookside road,
          whose dun decaying cover
              beds equally, hesitant
          or eager feet,
              whose trees'
                  absent leaves reveal
              their living skeletons—
and the whole
          of the brook's
              not so meandering life
flowing surely around,
or musically over
          each obstruction en route
              to the greater river
                      en route to ocean—
              brook whose populous
          fern ranks wither
      to invisible—as if
      they never existed,
as if their summer
      profligacy never
          greened the forest
              floor in faith
                  or temerity, as if
              no depth of snow
              could overthrow
          their spring
explosion—as if
      that single pleasure
          might pay
      for an eternity
of cold.

The Central Park Five

When I think of the boys
robbed of all

some of us take
for granted—

all five surviving,
emerging after torment

as compassionate men—
I think of Viktor Frankl.

I see again the *extras*
appended to the movie,

the miracle of each of them
transcending resentment—

the audience standing
their ovation,

tears streaking skins
of every color, hugs

making ones. I think
of the men's forgiveness,

and the Emanuel Church
families'—how theirs laid

a hundred-fifty-year
racist symbol to rest.

I hear again the men's
discovery, that telling

their story to such a reception,
and in service speaking

to students was healing.
I think of all of this

appended to the movie
as coda, as if

such greatness of spirit
were beside the point.

Knee-Deep

Among the raucous ralliers,
sat a man more still
than rest—a heron waiting
knee-deep in lake
among marauding gulls—

as the Narcissus
who would be king
made love to his own polemic
the people reflected
like whitewater.

The placid man
did not react on cue—
not cheering with his fellows,
not laughing, not waving
a sign, perhaps listening
intently to the speaker—

but more likely,
to some inner piper
inviting wandering—

not shouting agreement
or invective, as they all
were exhorted, not praising
his invisible clothes,
as the would-be emperor
spoke of all they should
fear and loathe—

the man's face
wore an expression
of hope that shone
like a lone flashlight
in a mansion
the lack of power
made dark.

Shift

Though I know I'm supposed
to applaud all pollinators,
including wasps invading my space,
dive-bombing outdoor meals,
nesting in eaves, hovering
in constant proximity—
I don't.

If my prejudice makes exception
for honeys and my garden's
most prolific bees—
for their fuzzy bobbing
and weaving, their bumbling
against delicate petals
which does no harm,

their lolling in summer breeze,
these gentle teddy bears of bees,
these yogis of everything stinging,
will that begin to shift
an ism in me?

I Could Be Driving

Shame on me for asking
a salesman based on fallacy:

the guy who sold you it
will care about the warranty.

Two years later,
Lennie's long gone—

maybe washing cars
or selling insurance.

So I tell Tony, my driver's seat
is tearing—*Your credit's good,*

I can put you
in a two-model up-grade

with air-conditioning,
eight dollars less per month,

a lot more car, what do you think?
I'm thinking, why did Lennie leave,

the seam's just beginning to tear—
then something clicks in my head:

I won't have to drive this beater
with a missing hubcap

where I smacked a curb,
the scratch where a passenger

kicked the dash, this living history
of my quotidian miseries.

I could be driving
a spanking new car,

impress my friends,
and win back my Ex.

Well yes, he admits,
the insurance and registration

cost more, and we ask
a down payment.

So I end up in auto-body,
where I *should* have gone,

where Frank says they don't mend.
So I get a whole new seat,

thinking, it's not really a tear—
but more of a pulling away.

Hedge

I have planted a green screen
between their constant urgency
and my Arcady, their noise-making need
of excessive speed—
                                    though my hedge
can't grow fast enough to please me,
and I travel the road as often as any,
knowing no garden will outlast
humanity's love of order:

I have driven by old lodgings
and seen the wrack and ruin
of all I once achieved,
                                    neglected, uprooted,
my every vestige desecrated—
we needn't even die to see
Eden lapsing back to wilderness
or desert without us, and yet—

we accept every proffered apple,
and persevere until death,
despite every evidence of irony.

April's Cream Scones, or: Saving April from Megalomania

Megalomania, because if I could bake and deliver enough at once, I'd rule the world with my cream scones—so, if you bake them yourselves, you'll save me from megalomania, and you from serfdom. Of course, the baking and delivering would mean keel-hauling a passel of minions, as I couldn't do it alone. Keelhauling's problematic, as I'd have to learn it. Do sailors who know still exist? I bet they'd beg to teach me, after eating a scone.

Finding minions isn't difficult. I'm sure I trip over them everywhere, though you have to know how to recognize them—only someone truly willing to "employ" minions will: it's a bit like pheromones. So, scratch minions. Would a *Fortune 500* company be big enough to get cream scones to *everyone*? I only want world domination if it includes everyone. Faux world domination would be worse than faux designer bags, because the everyone-excepts would know—it wouldn't just be me, carrying a faux bag with a faux-confident smirk.

What would a world ruled by April look like? Mandatory chocolate-consumption, for starters. "High tea" would become "chocolate high." Think how much sweeter we'd all be . . . I'm salivating just imagining—and you will, too—once you've eaten the scones. Does Pavlov ring a bell? Repeat after me: *Yes, April. Yes, anything, April.*

Eclipse

The restaurant dumpster's
fetid odors rose
in spring air, as a flock

of white-uniformed cooks,
elegant as swans
on the stained back stoop

in watery twilight,
held pin-holed paper,
cardboard lids, pie-tins,

projecting individual
eclipses. Bill, the line cook,
created a constellation—

Chef teased only two more
strategically placed,
would make a smiley face.

Jeffrey, the sous-chef,
and would-be scientist,
fashioned an actual

camera obscura:
shadow box with cut-out
lens and viewfinder

for obscuring,
as the waiter-cum-poet
gazed directly at the sun,

through a blank page's
single puncture—
chided, and guided

to project mere shadows
of the fantastic
on the concrete,

as she protested, *The radio
said to look through a pinhole—*
while inside, fine dining

continued: the faculty club's
susurration of forks
and explication of the obscure.

Figuratively Speaking

What lesson shall we glean
from beeches, who cling to their fading,
withering leaves all through winter,
like an apology for other trees' nudity;
their propensity for growing in groves
of their own society,
rustling in conversation
we can't yet translate—
though intuition whispers
against judgment
if we listen.

II

Dark Suite for My Country

I.

Dark as an overcast night,
licorice, ink, ravens, outer space.
Let me see the beauty
in crows mowing silence
like hundred rusty tractors,
or a crowd calling for murder—
and the peace in sleeping
in my closed eyes' night,
the safety in waking
in darkness none may penetrate.

II.

In darkness none may penetrate,
lies dark money without which
less corrupt politicians might win;
less partisan judges be anointed,
less partial justice apportioned;
and privilege be less limited—
none yet have proved it
can't be infinite as space-time,
or imagination or grace—so, give it
like sun gives light to everyone.

III.

Like sun gives light to everyone,
dark matter gives gravity to galaxies
that would otherwise fly apart
from centers no longer holding.
Say eighty-five percent of matter is dark,
named for not interacting with light,

for being invisible—which is not the same
except in dark skin color in America—
America, where we can do more than hope
for the energy to change.

IV.

For the energy to change,
look to dark: sixty-eight percent
of everything, its endless potential
permeates space, accelerates
universal expansion, peels galaxies
from each other like dividing cells,
begetting new galaxies,
as rogue planets and ejected stars
roam the empty outer spaces,
in the dark energy of infinite possibility.

V.

In the dark energy of infinite possibility,
let freedom ring, in the World Wide Web,
in the deep, and dark webs
allowing us to be anonymous
if we wish, independent, but connected,
not indexed by search engines
or police states, free to navigate
information, communication,
to salve trials and tribulation,
as dark humor makes light of dark matters.

VI.

As dark humor makes light of dark matters,
lave me with a soft summer night,
warm air alive with a symphony
of invisible insects we never knew
kept humans from going extinct,
bathe me in the scent of peonies
and roses, of fungus and bark, of earth,
and grasses I can only guess at,
in the silken dusk I don like lingerie,
as I lay me down to sleep,
dark as an overcast night.

Snowflakes

Call me *Snowflake,*
if I melt over innocence
or guilt, abortion or the death
penalty; if I weep over a sad
or happy movie, or anything in this
endless blizzard of division; if I love
anyone in the reality I choose
to believe, as snow piles in drifts
no one, right, or left,
can see above.

Call me *Snowflake,*
if I appreciate another's
beauty, or offer sympathy
to anyone in or outside my tribe,
or truly lisen for one prismatic
minute to one human trying
to climb the frozen snowbank
of my opinions.

The Blessings in Separation

Dearest, we are each free
to rule our own country,

to fence with evergreens
and perennials, instead

of legislation or barbed wire
and armed guards,

free to escape reality
in waking dreams,

or to make reality
of dreams, to conjure

a book or a degree
where none existed—

or to spin anxiety's
clinging web from seeming.

We are free
to meditate mindfully,

or work till we drop
from exhaustion, each free,

in our country of one,
from competing domestic

or ego needs,
free of any need

to cooperate, compromise,
or concede, free to be

each unadulterated me,
free of any benefits

of a union state: tax breaks,
shared gross or net product

or rainy day funds,
free of caretaking,

or a helpmate—
free to contemplate

the blessings in nearly
a generation of separation.

W ÷ E

equals the meanest

        common denominator

of me's

    a former whole

        number blown to smithereens

    radioactive factions

divided into fractions

    where a fractured me

        can subtract an other

in schools or stores

    or streets

        where the last one standing

    will have no party

no policy nor argument

        no division

    just exponential memories

of subtraction

        en route to zero

the Earth returned

to the birds and bees

who survive the heat

American Quarantine

Like the dripping of a tap . . .
    I cannot escape
plague's slight, insistent thunder.

No Matter What

My death is not a god
I hope to outwit,
nor a black hole
in a looming future
whose event horizon
I hope to escape—
but a daily possible reality,
an adventure
I may or may not engender
unwittingly or to wit.
My death is here with me,
no matter what I see,
a possible god
or collective conscious shift,
I will in one holistic moment,
surrender to,
like no one I ever loved.

The Knock-Knock Bardo

While I travel the world's
geography, history,
and virtual present,
in mind and poetry—
a September reality
knocks, constant
as a wound-up alarm clock,
startling me from work,
leisure, and sleep equally,
as if to remind me of the world
my body lives in, regardless
of metaphysical distractions—
the house over-spread
by the massive oak,
whose acorns slingshot
deck, and shotgun metal roof,
like Tolkien's angry Ents,
while the rest thud softly
onto lawn, as arrows into flesh.
Do I mistake as warfare,
an offered harvest
I thought belonged
to squirrels and chipmunks?
Should I contest
rodents' rights,
eye-to-avaricious-eye
on weeping sod,
snatch their manna
by the bushel,
cook up a way—
pan-seared or baked in cake—
to make acorns appetizing?
Am I meant to mind
the oak's business,
instead of what I thought

was mine, install
a nanny-cam to better spy?
Do I need to be outside,
attentively breathing
autumn air, and drinking
Chardonnay light
like a Buddhist Bacchus,
walking barefoot
on cool, dewy grass—
and bruising woody knobs,
to avert being unwittingly
slain in the spirit?
Shall I ask the oak
to favor me,
with a direct hit
on my foggy noggin,
to wake me
to the present present?

Whole

Pink mist, glowing snow,
why wound a new day's glory
with senseless breaking?

Peace Hymn for the Republic

My eyes have seen the gore in every battle of the hordes,
my heart knows all that swords achieve is breeding ever more,
but listening tends the vineyards where the grapes of peace are stored—
her truth is teaching us:

Glory be, in civility!
Glory be, in civility!
Glory be, in civility!
Her truth is teaching us.

I can hear a better future so content with harmony,
that no man or woman will deny our rhapsody,
intolerance will burn in fires of divinity.
Her love is changing us.

Glory be, in civility!
Glory be, in civility!
Glory be, in civility!
Her love is changing us.

She has sounded loud the trumpet that need blow for no more wars,
she'll learn to play jazz standards and throw open all the doors,
she'll welcome every one of us to dance forever more.
Her joy invites us in.

Glory be, in civility!
Glory be, in civility!
Glory be, in civility!
Her joy invites us in.

With hearts full of compassion that transfigures you and me;
let no one die to grow our souls, but live to make us free—
let every rainbowed nation dance and sing in harmony.
Our love unites us all.

Glory be, in civility!
Glory be, in civility!
Glory be, in civility!
Our love unites us all.

The Force

When I hear a giant,
Jack in the beanstalk creaking,
I think *tree* immediately,
but puzzle when it persists,
without a trace of wind.
I enter the woods cautiously,
with an eye on the canopy—
and witness, after maybe
eighty years of growing—
a top-heavy poplar, easing
slowly as an archly fainting
maiden down—then, suddenly
as an accident to ground—
with an awesome final display
of its ship's mast length
and emperor's girth—taking
smaller trees and limbs with it
like collateral proletariat,
or an ancient pharaoh buried
with sacrificial servants—
but more shocking is
this third witnessing in one month,
four fallen before me this year,
after a lifetime of none.
Trees growing peacefully
for longer lives than mine—
throwing themselves at my feet
with tons of literal force.
I don't mean this egotistically,
though any first person use
indicts: *Is it me*,
electrically, am I become
some awful god of falling trees?

How to Keep Your Head from Exploding

1) Rub two pencils together,
   until you've worn a saddle in each,
   exposing the graphite center.

2) Glue the saddle sides together,
   forming a cross.

3) Glue the cross to a blank page,
   hang it above your desk,
   and study it, all day if you wish.

4) Peel a head of cabbage carefully,
   so as not to tear any leaves.

5) Sew them together
   at the bottom ends
   in a circular fashion,
   forming a cabbage rose.

6) Consider the difference
   between it,
   and a real cabbage rose,
   why we make such distinctions.

7) Peel a cabbage rose carefully,
   so as not to tear any petals.

8) Glue the petals together, forming
   a faux head of cabbage.

9) Contemplate why we say
   a head of cabbage, how close
   you are to having one.

10) Think about why we say
    someone is *ahead of me.*

11) Tear the cross from the page,
    creating a ragged halo
    where some paper
    stays glued to the pencils.

12) Place the injured page on your desk,
    and use the cross to write about any
    or all of this. Take as long as you wish.

Juno's First Fly-By

I'm ready to visit Jupiter's
    blue north pole

I imagine awash
    in Soul—so used to storms,

he can't help but sing
    while he strums,

of wind and stinging sleet
    as god-sent destiny—

whose clouds have shadows
    some watery source

must shimmer under—
    whose rainbowed

southern aurora
    Juno recorded,

    along with his Alt-Blues,
    more ghostly or godly

than whale songs—
    a response to the call

we fear to make.
    NASA wants to know

if this gas giant's
    core is solid,

but I don't see either
    as static reality—

change, however slow,
    remains a universal constant.

If I hold my hitching thumb
    aloft to beckon Juno,

will she fly by for me,
    eager as she must be

for close-ups of her husband,
    even though his radiating fire

wards off touch—like you, my Love—
    like a virgin groom she must woo

for a millennium or two
    before they consummate.

From the Ruins

Today, from the ruined house
crumbling by the road,
where time and weather
slow-blasted a hole through the roof
exposing a bedroom, where no one
has slept in peace or otherwise
for an age, where somehow,
sun must have fingered through
second storey flooring,
first storey ceiling and floor,
to nurture an immigrant seed,
season after season,
while the once white house
decayed around it,
there rose unbeknownst to anyone,
a sapling that today
announced itself a graceful tree,
leafing its canopy
over the empty nest.

III

The City of Lost Shoes

I see them on roads,
   sidewalks, parking lots,

and beaches: mostly sandals,
   and flip-flops

in summery colors,

   some in pairs,
  but more often not—

I can't stop gnawing
   the obvious thought,

   as if my canines

need more grinding—
   I hope no soul

was kidnapped,

   losing a shoe in confusion—
  maybe one or two

   loosed them in fear of man,

or beast, or forgot them
   caught in the firesights

of greater loss:

   an immigrant watering
  a lakeshore mansion's garden,

   still hoping to move

his family to the country
   he once imagined

as providence;

   and two non-exempt
one-percenters,

   who dedicated

a pedestrian's bench
   to their twenty-six-year-old

dead son. Surely,

   all the beach kept were left
in the barefoot pleasure

   of sand's massage,

but I want *all*—every lonely,
   new or tattered shoe,

even those on burning roads,

   pocked and dusty shoulders—
to have shed,

   as bare soles

levitated from them,
   in rapture any prejudice

has yet to imagine.

Hunger Stones

You will see us—

    orangey-beige, overlaid

with brooding gray—

    pockmarked and scarred,

dated and aged—

    poems on sandstone,

carved on soft rocks,

    warning of hard times,

a paradox, ignored

    over centuries

of repeated history—

    you will see us

when droughts

    impoverish rivers

geology and climate

    made rich—

you will expose us

    more often as

you warm a world thirsting

for snow and rain,

as you burn

in the inferno

you made of Earth.

You will suffer us

when hunger

turns to greed

in the heedlessly rich,

and need,

in the needlessly poor,

when more of everything—

except love and compassion—

is the only creed

you heed with determination

or faith. *If you see me,*

weep. If you see me,

throw a stone

into the ocean

of apathy

and distraction—

build a cairn

to mark your highest road.

Wired

Wandering outside
simultaneously,

did awe unite them
like parents beholding

their firstborn, amazed
by their creation, a party

with people enough
to trip over and squeeze by—

were they really so desired
or friendly? They slid,

with identical sighs,
into matched blue rockers,

wired for the sound
or silence of each other's need.

Those moments I watched,
party noise clicked off,

as if my tuning made
that station vanish,

the world reducing
to one nation, which I was,

and was not a part of—
divided by a force-field

shimmering into sight,
as the party and I

spun dizzily,
in the atmosphere's

frail divide between us
and infinity—

while they were the axis
for better or worse.

Perhaps they glanced
at each other, or spoke

softly as a light rain
began to hallow

autumn leaves,
golden as the rule,

and the spirit
linking all of us.

Hypocritic Oath

If I believe in the sanctity
of lives, but make exceptions,
what does that make me?

Does my gut not putrefy
what I eat, do I not sneeze,
lie, and bleed?

If I only lie *socially*,
does that make me
superior to other liars?

Does the sun or moon
choose to shine
only on me and mine?

At the end of the revolution
marking another day with
or without soulful change,

we say the sun sets—
in rosy glory or hazy smog—
but in fact, we turn our backs on it.

Romantic, familial, conservative,
liberal, moderate, progressive,
independent, disaffected—

is it feasible to *do no harm*—
or should we qualify,
whenever possible?

If I unknowingly crush
or chop a bug while mowing,
or unconsciously judge

a soul based on color, politics,
gender, etcetera, do I not
harm equally as intent?

Do I not reek of hypocrisy,
miasmic as dung, as much
as any fellows I've deemed

insincere or mislead?
Since we can't bring back any dead,
or win forgiveness from any id—

shall we let our compass
be compassion, in this dim-lit grove
of groping branches

and exposed roots,
in this wilderness
of self-righteousness?

Pandemic Workout

Swimming in warm rain,
the heavens sob on shoulders,
balm for cold solitude.

Thought

A flock of crows inked the sky
like a Rorschach blot,

a thought bubble that rode
an unseen breeze aloft

while I watched, lost
as the novel I never wrote,

the crows twisting and turning,
changing direction and collective shape,

like the life I never expected
to write with every breath,

my body still its willing servant,
as whole nations rise and fall

in imagination, and I find the will
to progress, blot, by breath.

The Gift

I found time where I left it,
  though I didn't remember then.

Then, energy seemed like a gift
 my double somewhere

must have chosen to please me.
  If I chose a gift for myself,

it would be anything but ease—
  what fun's work or play

or anything fluid,
  without turbulence?

The gift of turbulence is
  the way it plays with gravity—

who doesn't want
  to undo gravity's buttons

and play with weightlessness,
  to see how being changes?

Why not spend some time
  and energy with pleasure,

learning to unbutton a minute
  so minutely, it matters?

The Beyond

To all the experiences
    I will not have had
in corporeal form—

parasailing, storm chasing,
    space flight, ejaculating—
rest ye all in peace.

I will be giddy to have gone
    beyond laundry, taxes, Tweets,
hangnails and corporate corruption,

police states, corpulent anxiety,
    corporal punishment—
and even past my corpus,

which will not delve as deep
    as one pollinating bee,
nor comfort me,

as one spoken word
    from my mother would—
nor be as brilliant

as even the smallest waterfall.
    I will, I hope, have gone
beyond my corpse,

but no one who knows
    is talking, and that is
as it should be.

Executor

We shake hands

      across the vortex,

visible only to me,

      as I imagine our next

investment office meeting.

      I take the card he hands me,

like a scorching brand—

      too hot for purse

or pocket—let it cool

      on polished oak.

I listen to him talk,

      as from a distance—

not across his desk,

      but from the other side

of the maelstrom

      roaring like a hurricane

toward me as I nod,

      pretending to pay attention

to the present, my mother

so calm and lovely

in autumn colors,

while I am drenched,

shivering from all

the salt water I anticipate

in my future execution

in the winter of our love.

Dear Attila

Hello, fellow snowbird,
with your second home

in Florida, in the city
next to my in-laws-to-be.

Thank you for the pre-flight
commiseration

over northern winters,
the mutual appreciation

of a southern break, for shared love
of certain books and movies.

Thank you for favoring me
with your dimples

and good cheer,
for your reluctance to hurt

with political dueling,
what you assumed must be

my liberal feelings
as a Vermonter.

Thank you for dipping
your toes in anyway,

for laving them
in perfectly civil debate

scaling walls,
for the concession

that both sides
have been known to lie,

for your self-deprecating humor
in referring to yourself

as being to the right
of Attila the Hun—

but disarming
and attempting to conquer

with charm instead
of your namesake's force,

for being so courteous
as to renew my faith

in the humanity
of those with whom

I disagree politically.

What Is Metaphor For?

For an hour, metaphor
is a shovel I dig fertile soil with,
            discarding rocks and clinging roots
                        I sever and remove, like lies

I'm weary of, but can't dispose of—
shifting them to fill
            another hollow or indentation
            my imagination's deemed unsightly,

disturbing a brown toad,
            who hops realistically away,
                        as I alter the shape
of another gardening station

            whose reality I plan
to level. I keep digging, thinking
I'll find truth and have
                        no further use for stories,

but truth is the hole I've dug, the hole
I've determined the depth of,
            the hole I'm free
to grow an imagined reality in.

Speaking of Being

How many steps
till the subfloor nail

beneath the rug popped—
stopping its holding job,

its knitting together
of unseen sinews

un-guessed by any
save the carpenter,

who revealed the mystery
to me—say it was

my eleventh step,
after uncounted years

wearing a woolen path
between bed and bathroom,

navigating in full moon light
on a night I otherwise

would never have remembered—
say it was the day

I stepped in to bring you tea
with honey to soothe

your sinus woes—
or some gray

November Wednesday
neither of us could recall

even if we wished,
a night or day like any

uncounted other—
except every step

on the nail after that
elicits a creaking

speaking of being
one step closer to the end

of a holding pattern.

Twenty-First Century Preamble

We the People
of the United States,
in order to form
a more perfect union
than chocolate
and coffee, or hotdogs
and baseball—
of liberty and justice
for all: for donkeys,
elephants, and cats
who walk by themselves—
but depend equally
on common love
and compassion—
we establish equality,
to ensure domestic tranquility—
even for the braying,
trumpeting, yowling
fat cats, politicians, pundits,
masses, and middle class,
with whom still others
may disagree; we do provide
for the common defense,
which is not synonymous
with offense or pre-emption,
to promote the common welfare
of every human being,
and secure the blessings
of health, education, and wealth
without prejudice to all,
to ensure posterity measured
by the Golden Rule, polished
to its highest gloss;
we do ordain and establish,
in common sense, honoring

our common divinity—
in the United States of America,
and globally, a model,
and beacon of hope, beckoning
to the oppressed everywhere.
We enshrine this Constitution,
this covenant of cooperation,
in civility, independence,
and interdependence,
the preservation of which
will make America great again.

Corridors

A shared office space might employ one for privacy or primacy, as might a prison. A house with many rooms might require one for ingress, unless it were open concept, a cathedral-ceilinged communal space to prepare for grace, with faith in some return, for coming and going in blessedness. Another kind might run rings around a fear that built a fortress. Another might allow other countries or land-owners narrow access. But in this quantum present, let us agree: No more barbed wire still retaining trace DNA, though no flesh or blood remains in sight. No more fortified trenches filled with soldiers, no more corridors of war. No fearful corridors of any sort, for lonely ghosts to float—let them go into the great unknown, let every such corridor be buried in everlasting snows and forgotten, or opened into fields any flowers or passersby may occupy. Let no land, no thing, and no one be owned, or let possession be ten tenths of the law, but let the only law be kindness.

Epithalamium

While the resident doe and fawn
dine on our green field—

to which they may have greater claim—
I hear with my chest, then feet,

the morning train's whistle
moaning through the river's fog,

like a new love I should greet,
like a bell tolling for me to attend

some unknown sacrament,
the bass rumble of each passing car

vibrating my cello from head to toes,
strumming each taut string

with ineffable meaning,
calling me to go I know not where,

to leave a multitude of beauties
I would not abandon—

not least, the our
of these blessed hours—

not just the house:
and ground,

but the home I know
wherever you are.

State of the Union Aubade

Moving through dawn's ethereal twilight gray,
as darkness leaches from valley landscape,

passing gold-lit rooms like staged plays; wombs
from which a day's labor is born, brief havens

for waking—one man with his back to me,
though he doesn't know it, bent like a lover

to his task, with faith in walls that may not
be all he needs to survive catastrophe—

one man with his hand cupped so tenderly
around a mug, I want to hug him—

maybe contemplating ways to face the day
with faith in compassion—and adversity—

each luminous, breakable neighbor
sipping hot coffee or eating a donut,

wholly in the moments duty soon will co-opt,
but none more—or less divine, than any other.

Author's Bio

April Ossmann is author of *Event Boundaries* (awarded
a Vermont Arts Council Creation Grant, and a Vermont
Book Award finalist), and *Anxious Music* (both from Four
Way Books); and has published poetry widely in journals
and anthologies. A former executive director of Alice
James Books, she owns a poetry consulting business (www.
aprilossmann.com), offering manuscript editing, publishing
advice, tutorials, and workshops, and taught at the low-
residency MFA in Creative Writing Program at Sierra
Nevada College. She lives in White River Junction, Vermont.

www.ingramcontent.com/pod-product-compliance
Lightning Source LLC
Jackson TN
JSHW022309170425
82815JS00008B/14